Deck Barge Safety

U.S. Department of Labor

Occupational Safety and Health Administration

OSHA 3358 01N
2009

I0473842

Contents

Introduction

This document presents guidance on preventing injuries and illnesses from workplace hazards on deck barges.[1] Approximately 4,000 deck barges operate in the United States, using different types of winches and other equipment in a variety of operations.[2]

Employees on these vessels can face serious hazards. Between 1997 and 2006, 305 employees were killed on barge/tow combinations, and 379 explosions or fires occurred on barges or towboats, killing 14 employees.[3] Some examples of these incidents are:

- An employee was setting a steel pile upright in the water. The steel pile was being held upright by a chain connecting it to the barge. A large boat passed by the barge, creating a wake. The barge moved and the steel pile fell, pivoting on the chain. The steel pile struck the employee on the back of the head, killing him.

- An employee carrying a right angle grinder attempted to step from one barge to another by using a barge rope. He lost his balance and fell into the river between the two barges. He was not wearing a life vest. Rescue efforts were unsuccessful and the employee drowned.

- An employee was standing on a barge with a coworker, waiting for a personnel basket to land on the barge. He was holding a small sheet of plywood. He stepped back, stumbled on a board, and fell over the side of the barge into 12 feet of water. He was not wearing a life vest. Rescue attempts by his coworkers with a life ring failed and he drowned.

- An employee on a pile-driving barge was directed to put up a ladder and get survey equipment off a breasting dolphin. A short time later, a coworker and the foreman heard splashes and

[1] A deck barge is a manned or unmanned barge that has a continuous, flat main deck. It is used to carry deck cargo and is also used in the marine construction industry for such work as pier or bulkhead construction, dredging, bridge construction and maintenance, and marine oil service. These types of vessels are not self-propelled.

[2] American Waterway Operators cited in National Transportation Safety Board, *Fire Aboard Construction Barge Athena 106, West Cote Blanche Bay. Louisiana*, October 12, 2006. http://www.ntsb.gov/publictn/2007/MAR0701.pdf.

[3] Coast Guard data cited in National Transportation Safety Board, *Fire Aboard Construction Barge Athena 106, West Cote Blanche Bay. Louisiana*, October 12, 2006. http://www.ntsb.gov/publictn/2007/MAR0701.pdf.

another employee saw the first employee go under the rake of the barge, where he became trapped. He then surfaced and was carried by the current into some pilings. He was rescued by two coworkers in a john boat and taken to the local emergency room, where he later died.

- Three employees entered a tank on a barge. The tank did not contain sufficient oxygen. One employee died and the other two required hospitalization.

- Two riggers were capping a sulfur well in a shallow bay, working from the deck of a barge equipped with a crane with a clamshell bucket. The employees dug around the well casing and then set a caisson around the wellhead. Standard procedures required them to cut off the casing and then weld a circular plate over the end. The first employee went into the caisson to wrap a sling around the pipe end, and was asphyxiated due to hydrogen sulfide gas. The second employee entered the caisson to rescue him, and was also overcome by the gas. Neither was wearing respiratory protection (i.e., airline or Self-Contained Breathing Apparatus). Both employees died.

- A deckhand was working on a spud barge helping a coworker raise the spud legs using a winch system. A 42-inch pin was to be inserted into the spud leg to prevent it from falling if the winch brake released. The spud leg was raised just high enough for the employee to insert about 4 inches of the pin into the hole, when the winch brake failed. The pin came up and the employee was pinned between the pin and spud leg, sustaining fatal crushing injuries to his chest.

- A towing vessel was pushing two deck barges to a pile-driving location off the Louisiana coast. While the vessels were underway, a spud on one of the barges suddenly dropped into the water from its raised position. The spud struck and ruptured a buried high-pressure natural gas pipeline. The gas ignited and created a fireball that engulfed the towing vessel and both barges. The master of the towing vessel and four barge employees were killed, and one barge employee was listed as missing.

Many such injuries and deaths could be prevented with proper controls, procedures, training, and awareness of hazards and possible solutions. On the following pages the major physical hazards of concern are highlighted and steps to address them are outlined, along with resources for additional information.

Regulation of Workplace Safety on Deck Barges

For construction barges underway and other "uninspected vessels," the U.S. Coast Guard oversees fire and lifesaving equipment and overall navigational matters. Its regulations for uninspected vessels are found in the Code of Federal Regulations, 46 CFR Part 25:

- Life Preservers and Other Lifesaving Equipment [46 CFR 25.25]
- Fire Extinguishing Equipment [46 CFR 25.30]
- Backfire Flame Control [46 CFR 25.35]
- Ventilation [46 CFR 25.40]

The U.S. Occupational Safety and Health Administration (OSHA) exercises its authority to regulate employers for all working conditions not covered by U.S. Coast Guard regulations on these vessels, provided that the vessel is in the geographic jurisdiction of OSHA.

OSHA regulations that apply are in 29 CFR Part 1910, with the following exceptions:

- For ship repair, shipbuilding, and shipbreaking, 29 CFR Part 1915 standards apply.
- For longshoring and cargo handling operations, 29 CFR Parts 1918 and 1919 standards apply.
- For marine construction activities, 29 CFR Part 1926 standards apply.

OSHA standards can be found at www.osha.gov.

For a detailed explanation of OSHA jurisdiction, see OSHA Instruction CPL 2-1.20 November 8, 1996, *OSHA/U.S. Coast Guard Authority Over Vessels.* http://www.osha.gov/pls/oshaweb/owadisp.show_document?p_table=DIRECTIVES&p_id=1526.

Note: CPL 2-1.20 is to be replaced with a new instruction, · entitled: *OSHA Authority Over Vessels and Facilities on U.S. Navigable Waters and the Outer Continental Shelf;* effective date TBD.

Slips, Trips and Falls

Slips, trips and falls are major causes of workplace injuries in the maritime industry and can lead to overboard incidents.

- A slip occurs when the foot skids, usually on a wet or slippery surface (e.g., ice) and the person falls backward or forward.
- A trip occurs when an obstacle stops the foot and the person falls forward.
- Same-level falls can be the result of an unrecoverable slip or trip. Another type of same-level fall is a step and fall, when the front foot lands on a surface that is lower than expected. In this type of fall, the person usually falls forward.
- Elevated falls include falls from stairs, equipment, ladders, and falls through holes in decks, and uncovered or unguarded hatches.

Many factors can contribute to slips, trips, and falls on a barge. Some of these are gear and equipment on the deck, changing walking speed or direction, slippery surfaces (oil, ice and snow), fatigue, carrying heavy objects, visibility, and unsuitable footwear.

Minimizing Hazards on Deck[4]

- Keep all walking and working surfaces clean, dry, and unobstructed.
- Keep all areas free of debris.

[4]Adapted from American Waterways Operators Interregion Safety Committee, *Lesson Plan for Slip, Trip and Fall Prevention,* November 2002. http://www.americanwaterways.com/commitment_safety/slpsplan.doc.

- Clean up and/or report any spill immediately.
- Stack materials in a stable manner.
- Secure gear and equipment that is not in use.
- Keep stairs, doorways, walkways, and gangways free of equipment and stowed materials.
- Secure ramps during loading and offloading operations.
- Repair leaks from hoses, pipelines, and valves immediately.
- Use non-skid protective deck compound and do not paint over the non-skid compound with standard paint.
- Have de-icing procedures in place when necessary.
- Paint the perimeter and tripping hazards in a contrasting color.

Precautions in Walking
- Walk at a normal rate, keeping your hands out of your pockets.
- Slow down when moving between different surfaces.
- Do not run.
- Minimize short stops.
- Avoid sharp turns.
- Modify your way of walking to match the surface, such as an icy deck.
- Do not jump from one barge to another.
- Do not climb on cargo, supplies, or equipment instead of using a ladder.
- Do not step on hatch covers.
- Avoid walking along the unguarded edge of a barge.
- Watch out for reduced visibility due to poor lighting and weather conditions. If working at night, be sure there is adequate illumination (e.g., flashlight, headlight, light tower).

Wearing Appropriate Footgear
- Wear safety shoes or boots with slip-resistant soles as appropriate.
- Keep shoes clean of mud, snow, ice, spilled liquids, and debris.

Preventing Elevated Falls
- Always maintain three-points of contact on a ladder—two hands

and a foot, or two feet and a hand—so that only one limb is in motion at any one time.

- Avoid overextending the body when performing tasks such as checking sounders, checking lights, and wiring rigging, which can lead to falls from ladders.

- Falls from portable ladders are one of the leading causes of occupational fatalities and injuries. Use the following safe work practices when using ladders:

  - Use ladders only for their designed purpose (i.e., step ladders should not be used as portable rung ladders).

  - Position the ladder so that for every four feet in height, the ladder extends out from the vertical surface at the base approximately one foot.

  - Make sure that the ladder is long enough for the job—if used for access to an upper landing surface the side rails must extend at least three feet above that surface.

  - Make sure that there is proper footing to keep the ladder from slipping or sliding.

  - Tie the ladder to a secure object. Remember that the vessel(s) that the ladder is secured to can move. Use the buddy system, if possible, so that one person can hold the ladder to stop it from moving.

  - Never use portable metal ladders near energized electrical equipment (such as conductors or electric arc welding machines).

  - Keep your body near the middle of the step and always face the ladder while climbing.

  - Do not move, shift, or extend ladders while in use. Move the ladder instead of stretching or leaning to the side to reach your work.

  - Use hand lines or a tool bag/belt to keep hands free when using a ladder.

  - Fully enclosed slip-resistant footwear should always be worn when using ladders.

- An adequate guard rail should be installed or employees should wear Personal Fall Arrest Systems when work is being performed above a solid surface (e.g., to prevent falls from the barge to the dock).[5]

[5]Effective January 1, 1998, body belts are not acceptable as part of a personal fall arrest system. See 29 CFR 1926.502(d) and 29 CFR 1915.159.

- Use gangplanks with guardrails to prevent falls on the dock or pilings.
- All deck holes, openings, and hatches should be covered or guarded.
- Pigeon holes should not be used to access barge walking or working surfaces.

For More Information About Preventing Slips, Trips and Falls

OSHA Safety and Health Topics: Fall Protection
http://www.osha.gov/SLTC/fallprotection/index.html.

OSHA Safety and Health Topics: Walking/Working Surfaces
http://www.osha.gov/SLTC/walkingworkingsurfaces/solutions.html.

OSHA Shipyard Employment eTool: Working Conditions—
Housekeeping http://www.osha.gov/SLTC/etools/shipyard/standard/
working_conditions/housekeeping.html.

OSHA Quick Card: Portable Ladder Safety Tips
http://www.osha.gov/Publications/portable_ladder_qc.html.

Falling Overboard

Personal Flotation Devices

If the deck of a barge or work platform is not equipped with an OSHA-compliant railing system, employees walking or working on deck must wear a U.S. Coast Guard-approved life jacket or buoyant work vest, also called a life preserver or personal flotation device

(PFD). These PFDs should be fully buckled, snapped, or zipped whenever there is a hazard of falling into the water, regardless of the size of the barge. While a PFD is not required to be worn while an employee is inside an enclosed cab or equipment compartment on a barge, each employee should have a PFD accessible to them at all times. This safety precaution will allow employees the opportunity to don a PFD in a reasonable amount of time during an emergency (i.e., vessel sinking, fire, etc.).

U.S. Coast Guard Regulations for Uninspected Vessels

Life Preservers and Other Lifesaving Equipment [46 CFR 25.25]

a. An approved and readily available PFD is required to be on board the vessel for each individual on board. An immersion/ exposure suit is considered to be an acceptable substitute for a PFD. All lifesaving equipment designed to be worn is required to be readily available and in serviceable condition.

b. Each vessel 26 feet or longer must have at least one approved ring life buoy which is immediately available. All lifesaving equipment designed to be thrown into the water is required to be immediately available and in serviceable condition.

c. An approved commercial hybrid PFD is acceptable if: worn when the vessel is underway and the intended wearer is not within an enclosed space; labeled for use on uninspected commercial vessels; and used as marked and in accordance with the owner's manual.

d. An approved light is required for all PFDs and immersion/ exposure suits. Also, all PFDs must have approved retro-reflective material installed.

Regular Maintenance and Inspection

Barges should be inspected by employers on a regular basis and as necessary, to prevent problems related to missing equipment, hazardous working surface conditions, and mechanical failures that could contribute to falls overboard. For example, inspections should check for missing or damaged PFDs, missing lifelines, and burned-out lights.

Safety Precautions

There are several controls that may help prevent employees from falling overboard. Examples include marking the edge of the deck with contrasting paint or, if practical, installing guardrails or handrails.

Job Hazard Analysis to Prevent Overboard Incidents

To reduce the risks of overboard incidents and drowning, employers and employees can conduct a joint job hazard analysis to identify conditions that may contribute to overboard incidents. Appropriate control measures and training can be implemented to reduce the hazards associated with falling overboard. For example, if the separation between a barge and the dock or another vessel is more than 12 inches, a gangway or ladder must be used. Additionally, it is important to look for warning signs such as employee fatigue, complacency, and lack of concentration, and resolve these issues before an overboard incident occurs. Employers also may consider hiring a professional safety engineer to evaluate hazards and possible controls.

Man Overboard Rescue Procedures

It is critical to have clear procedures in place in case someone falls overboard. Man-overboard procedures should incorporate the use of stand-by boats, life rings with appropriate length of rope (90 feet minimum), and ladders that extend three feet below and above the water surface. In a case where an employee falls overboard, they will need assistance to get back on board. This must be accomplished quickly, particularly if the water is frigid, the person is not wearing a life jacket, is tangled in a line or caught in a current. Crews should practice man overboard drills regularly. Additionally, in regions such as Alaska, where employees are at a greater risk of hypothermia, additional precautions (e.g., use of immersion suits) should be considered when there is a chance of falling overboard.

For More Information About Preventing Overboard Incidents

The American Waterways Operators. F*all Overboard Prevention Best Practices.* March 2001. http://www.americanwaterways.com/commitment_safety/BESTPRAC.doc.

The photograph (right) shows a spud without its securing pin inserted. This is an unsafe position and an example of an equipment hazard.

The photograph (left) shows a spud with its securing pin inserted. The spud is in a safe position and limits possible injuries due to equipment hazards.

Machinery and Equipment Hazards

Hazards related to the use of machinery and equipment can result in injuries to hands, feet, or limbs that become caught in moving machinery; head and other injuries from being struck by falling objects or moving equipment; and burns. Other potential hazards include getting pinned under a load; falling off equipment; and electric shock.

To reduce hazards from machinery and equipment:

- Inspect all equipment before use.
- Maintain equipment properly. Shut down and lockout the power source before repairing mechanical systems. Make repairs according to the manufacturer's guidelines.
- Ensure that the person using the equipment is trained in its proper use and maintenance.

- Install appropriate rails, temporary or permanent, to avoid equipment being driven off the barge or dock.
- Ensure retaining pins are properly installed and positively secured with a keeper or locking device.
- Emergency shut-offs must be easily accessible, and sufficient guarding should be used for equipment controls.

Hoists, Cranes and Derricks[6]

Hazards of hoists include being struck by a heavy object, such as the boom or the load being moved. To reduce these hazards:

- Stay clear when a hoist is being used unless you are part of the procedure and, in which case, never stand under a load or boom with a suspended load.
- Wear personal protective equipment, such as head, foot, eye, and hand protection at all times.
- Assess the hoisting systems for structural soundness by inspecting regularly for problems with welds, rivets, chains, pulleys, lines, blocks, hooks, etc.
- Secure power blocks with a safety chain.
- Ensure that cranes in use are secured to the barge.
- Do not try to help lift a load being hoisted.

Photograph of a spud winch, which assists in the raising and lowering of spuds on deck barges.

[6]Adapted from Nova Scotia Fisheries Sector Council, *Fish Safe: A Handbook for Commercial Fishing and Agriculture*, 2004.

Winches

Operating or working near winches may potentially expose employees to hazards such as body parts caught in a winch drum, being struck by a broken line or cable, and tripping over a line or cable.

- Use a device or tool, never your hand, to keep the winch line spooling properly.
- Enclose the winch drum in a cage if practical.
- Stay off the deck unless you are part of the operation.
- Never stand in, on, over, or in line with lines or cables connected to winches when they are under tension. The danger zone lies within 15 degrees of either side of a line under tension.
- Never step on or walk over the winch drum.
- Inspect the winch system regularly for problems associated with general or localized deterioration, cracked welds, and other structural, mechanical, or electrical deficiencies.
- Inspect lines and cable systems regularly, including blocks, hooks, and associated components, for signs of damage or deterioration.
- A guard should be installed between the winch operator and the connected cables to protect the operator from potential whiplash.
- Never stand in the bight of a line.

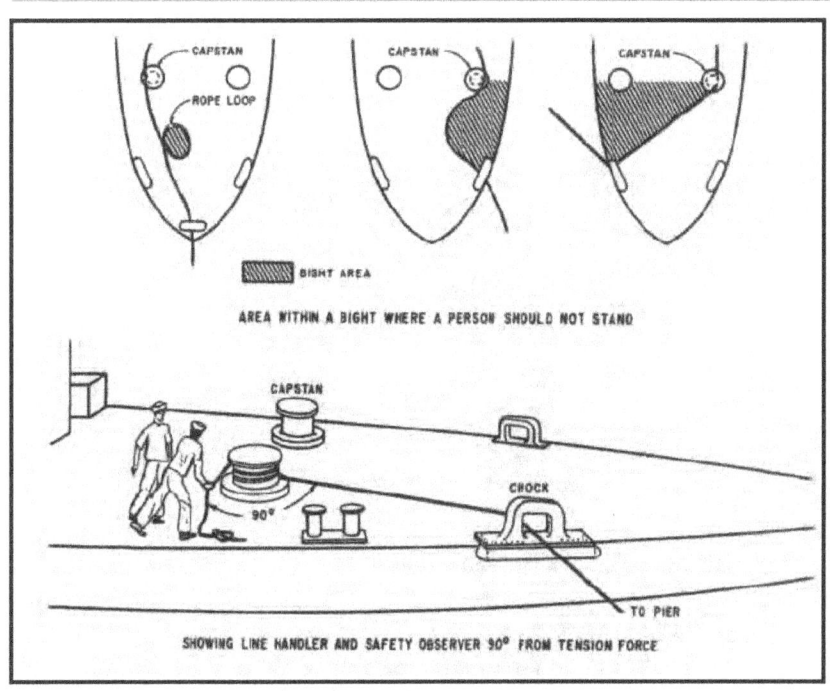

AREA WITHIN A BIGHT WHERE A PERSON SHOULD NOT STAND

SHOWING LINE HANDLER AND SAFETY OBSERVER 90° FROM TENSION FORCE

For More Information About Machinery and Equipment Safety

OSHA Shipyard Employment eTool: Gear and Equipment for Rigging and Materials Handling. http://www.osha.gov/SLTC/etools/shipyard/standard/material_handling/index_mh.html.

OSHA Publication, *Mobile Crane Inspection Guidelines for OSHA Compliance Officers,* June 1994. http://www.osha.gov/SLTC/cranehoistsafety/mobilecrane/mobilecrane.html

Hazards Associated with Confined/Enclosed Spaces

Photograph of proper signage used to indicate the designation of an enclosed or confined space.

The Confined or enclosed spaces on barges may have an atmosphere that is unsafe, causing injury or death. The main hazards include: oxygen deficiency, explosive or flammable atmospheres, and atmospheres containing toxic compounds. These hazards might be found in watertight compartments or other areas with little or no ventilation.

An oxygen-deficient atmosphere inside a tank can be caused by many factors. One example is rusting that may occur in a steel tank where water or water vapor is present. If the tank is airtight, as they are designed to be, then the rusting process would remove oxygen from the tank atmosphere until there is not enough oxygen in the space to support human life. Another example is displacement of oxygen by another gas or vapor, which may occur when a tank is sealed after it is freshly painted. The paint coating may not have time to cure, resulting in the paint vapor displacing oxygen.

An explosive or flammable atmosphere can develop from many sources. Some examples of these sources may include:

- If you are leasing a barge, a previous user may have dumped waste into the space or used it as a slop tank.
- A spill of diesel fuel or gasoline on deck may have entered the tank, resulting in an explosive atmosphere.

- The paint or coating system applied to the tank could ignite if not locally removed prior to hotwork.

Before beginning work in, near or around a confined space or compartment, a visual inspection must first be performed in order to identify potential physical, atmospheric and fire hazards. Second, the atmosphere must be tested, using a combustible gas meter, not only prior to entry into the space but also if you plan on doing hotwork on a tank exterior. Conducting hotwork on the exterior of a tank can be just as dangerous as when done internally if an explosive atmosphere or a flammable coating is present, which could result in a fire or explosion.

Toxic atmospheres are generally the most difficult to identify and can only be determined through testing, which should only be conducted by a qualified person (i.e., marine chemist, competent person, etc.). The potential for a toxic atmosphere is always present and can come from several sources including:

- A space that is painted and sealed up before the paint has time to cure, causing the off-gassing of the fresh paint to release toxic levels of paint and solvent vapors into the secured space.
- A tank cover inadvertently left open that allows nearby engine exhaust to raise the amount of carbon monoxide in the tank to dangerous levels.
- Contents from a chemical spill (deck above) entering the space.
- Multiple waste or slop dumped into a space that creates a toxic compound.

Based on the hazards discussed above, entry into any confined/enclosed space or any space with limited ventilation space on a deck barge should be done with caution.

Photograph shows an employee entering a confined space.

For More Information About Atmospheric Hazards and Confined Spaces

OSHA Safety and Health Topics: Confined Spaces
http://www.osha.gov/SLTC/confinedspaces/index.html.

Shipyard Employment e-Tool: Ship Repair
http://www.osha.gov/SLTC/etools/shipyard/shiprepair/sr_index.html.

Fire Hazards

A Steps that can be taken to prevent fires on board a barge include the following:[7]

- Store engine fuel tanks and compressed gas tanks properly, away from sources of ignition. Only keep onboard quantities of flammable and combustible materials that are necessary for operations and maintenance. Post appropriate danger signs.
- When dealing with work that is capable of providing a source of ignition through a flame or spark (hotwork), such as welding, cutting, burning, drilling, grinding, etc., follow these precautions:
  - Ensure the space is properly tested by a qualified or shipyard-competent person and deemed safe before work is begun. (See 29 CFR 1915.7 and 1915.15.)

    29 CFR 1915.7 – http://www.osha.gov/pls/oshaweb/owadisp. show_document?p_table=STANDARDS&p_id=10215

    29 CFR 1915.15 – http://www.osha.gov/pls/oshaweb/ owadisp.show_document?p_table=STANDARDS&p_id= 10221

[7]Adapted from Nova Scotia Fisheries Sector Council, *Fish Safe: A Handbook for Commercial Fishing and Aquaculture,* 2004. http://www.gov.ns.ca/lwd/healthand-safety/ docs/FishSafe.pdf and The American Waterways Operators Interregion Safety Committee, *Lesson Plan for American Waterways Operators/National Fire Protection Association/National Safety Council Hot Work Safety Brochure,* March 2002. http://www.americanwater ways.com/commitment_safety/HOTWORK.doc.

- Make sure that proper fire extinguishing equipment is near the work area and that it is maintained in a state of readiness for emergency use.
- Do not leave oxygen or acetylene hoses unattended.
- Consider where sparks will fall when doing hotwork and employ a fire watch.
- Shield fuel sources to protect them from ignition sources.
- Cover openings to prevent sparks from entering.
- Stop any hotwork if you smell fuel or gas until the source has been identified and the problem fixed.
- When welding or burning on the deck of a barge, the space below should be inspected to ensure that no flammable atmosphere or combustible materials are present.
- Use good housekeeping practices to limit the amount of clutter, debris and combustible/ flammable material.

Follow these safety measures to help prevent electrical fires:

- Make sure that electrical systems are installed by a qualified marine electrician and that electrical systems are inspected regularly.
- Regularly conduct visual inspections of connections, switches and wiring, which may be subject to corrosion from saltwater and damage from use.

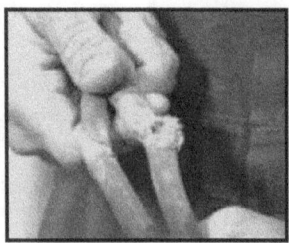 

Photos showing damaged wiring that could cause an electrical fire if used.

U.S. Coast Guard Regulations for Uninspected Vessels

Fire Extinguishing Equipment [46 CFR 25.30]

a. Hand-portable fire extinguishers and semi-portable fire extinguishing systems must be of the "B" type (i.e., suitable for extinguishing fires involving flammable liquids, greases, etc.).

b. Hand-portable fire extinguishers and semi-portable fire extinguishing systems must have a metal name plate listing the name of the item, rated capacity (gallons, quarts or pounds), name and address of person/firm for whom approved, and the manufacturer's identifying mark.

c. Portable fire extinguishers must be inspected and weighed every six months.

d. Minimum number of B-II hand-portable fire extinguishers required to be on board motor vessels: one if less than 50 tons, two if 50-100 tons, three if 100-500 tons, six if 500-1,000 tons, and eight if over 1,000 tons.

e. Fixed fire extinguishing systems must be an approved carbon dioxide type and must meet U.S. Coast Guard requirements. (See OSHA Directive CPL 02-01-020, November 1996.)

Backfire Flame Control [46 CFR 25.35]

Every gasoline engine installed after April 25, 1940, except outboard motors, shall be equipped with an acceptable means of backfire flame control.

Ventilation [46 CFR 25.40]

Fuel tanks and engine spaces, using fuel with a flashpoint of 110 degrees Fahrenheit or less, must be provided with adequate ventilation to remove explosive or flammable gases from the fuel tank compartment and bilges.

For More Information About Fire Hazards

OSHA Shipyard Employment eTool: Fire Protection
http://www.osha.gov/dcsp/products/etools/shipyard/fire_protection/
index.html.

Training

Many OSHA standards require employers to train employees in the safety and health aspects of their jobs. Other OSHA standards make it the employer's responsibility to limit certain job assignments to employees who are certified, competent, or qualified —that is, to employees who have received training either on-site or off-site. Designated personnel are selected or assigned by the employer or the employer's representative as being qualified to perform specific duties. Training is an essential part of every employer's safety and health program for protecting employees from injuries and illnesses.

To control or eliminate any hazards or other exposure to illness or injury, employees must be trained in the recognition and avoidance of unsafe conditions and the regulations applicable to their work environment. Some of the topics to be addressed in training for employees on deck barges are:

- Employee Emergency Plans
- Medical Services and First Aid

- Explosive and Other Dangerous Atmospheres
- Fire Protection and Prevention
- Handling and Storage of Materials
- Machinery and Machine Guarding
- Toxic and Hazardous Substances
- Storage of Gases and Fuels
- Gear and Equipment for Rigging and Material Handling
- Tools and Related Equipment
- Stairways and Ladders
- Fall Protection
- Work on or in the Vicinity of Radar and Radio
- Electrical Safety-Related Work Practices
- The Control of Hazardous Energy (Lockout/Tagout)
- Personal Protective Equipment
- Procedures for Securing Barges to Tugs
- Noise and Hearing Conservation

The training should address the specific hazards faced by employees on barges such as:

- Employee training should include ways to prevent overboard incidents. This includes use of personal flotation devices, as well as awareness of the risks of carelessness/distractions while working on deck or overextending oneself.
- Training on employee emergency plans must include man overboard rescue procedures and drills.
- Training for spud winch operators must include the use of spud securing pins before a barge is moved to a different worksite.[8]

One way to determine the content of training activities is to conduct a Job Hazard Analysis (Job Safety Analysis). This is a procedure for studying and recording each step of a job, identifying existing or potential hazards, and determining the best way to perform the job in order to reduce or eliminate the hazards. Information obtained from a Job Hazard Analysis can be used as the content for the training activities.

[8]U.S. Department of Labor, Occupational Safety and Health Administration, Spud Barge Safety Fact Sheet.

For More Information About Training

U.S. Department of Labor, Occupational Safety and Health Administration. *Job Hazard Analysis.* OSHA Publication 3071, http://www.osha.gov/Publications/osha3071.pdf Revised 2002.

U.S. Department of Labor, Occupational Safety and Health Administration, *Training Requirements in OSHA Standards and Training Guidelines* - OSHA Publication No. 2254, http://www.osha.gov/Publications/2254.html.

References

The American Waterways Operators. *Safety Tools/Documents Library.* http://www.americanwaterways.com/ commitment_safety/index.html.

Nova Scotia Fisheries Sector Council. *Fish Safe: A Handbook for Commercial Fishing and Aquaculture,* 2004. http://www.gov.ns.ca/lwd/healthandsafety/docs/FishSafe.pdf.

Occupational Safety and Health Administration. *OSHA Assistance for the Maritime Industry.* http://www.osha.gov/dts/maritime/index.html.

OSHA Assistance

OSHA can provide extensive help through a variety of programs, including technical assistance about effective safety and health programs, state plans, workplace consultations, voluntary protection programs, strategic partnerships, training and education, and more. An overall commitment to workplace safety and health can add value to your business, to your workplace, and to your life.

Safety and Health Program Management Guidelines

Effective management of employee safety and health protection is a decisive factor in reducing the extent and severity of work-related injuries and illnesses and their related costs. In fact, an effective safety and health program forms the basis of good employee protection, can save time and money, increase productivity and reduce employee injuries, illnesses, and related workers' compensation costs.

To assist employers and employees in developing effective safety and health programs, OSHA published recommended Safety and Health Program Management Guidelines (54 *Federal Register* (16): 3904-3916, January 26, 1989). These voluntary guidelines can be applied to all places of employment covered by OSHA.

The guidelines identify four general elements critical to the development of a successful safety and health management system:

- Management leadership and employee involvement,
- Worksite analysis,
- Hazard prevention and control, and
- Safety and health training.

The guidelines recommend specific actions, under each of these general elements, to achieve an effective safety and health program. The Federal Register notice is available online at www.osha.gov.

State Programs

The Occupational Safety and Health Act of 1970 (OSH Act) encourages states to develop and operate their own job safety and health plans. OSHA approves and monitors these plans. Twenty-four states, Puerto Rico, and the Virgin Islands currently operate approved state plans: 22 cover both private and public (state and local government) employment; Connecticut, New Jersey, New York, and the Virgin Islands cover the public sector only. States and territories with their own OSHA-approved occupational safety and health plans must adopt standards identical to, or at least as effective as, the Federal OSHA standards.

Consultation Services

Consultation assistance is available on request to employers who want help in establishing and maintaining a safe and healthful workplace. Largely funded by OSHA, the service is provided at no cost to the employer. Primarily developed for smaller employers with more hazardous operations, the consultation service is delivered by state governments employing professional safety and health consultants. Comprehensive assistance includes an appraisal of all mechanical systems, work practices, and occupational safety and health hazards of the workplace and all aspects of the employer's present job safety and health program. In addition, the service offers assistance to employers in developing and implementing an effective safety and health program. No penalties are proposed or citations issued for hazards identified by the consultant. OSHA provides consultation assistance to the employer with the assurance that his or her name and firm and any information about the workplace will not be routinely reported to OSHA enforcement staff.

Under the consultation program, certain exemplary employers may request participation in OSHA's Safety and Health Achievement Recognition Program (SHARP). Eligibility for participation in SHARP includes receiving a comprehensive consultation visit, demonstrating exemplary achievements in workplace safety and health by abating all identified hazards, and developing an excellent safety and health program.

Employers accepted into SHARP may receive an exemption from programmed inspections (not complaint or accident investigation inspections) for a period of 1 year. For more information concerning consultation assistance, see OSHA's website at www.osha.gov.

Voluntary Protection Programs (VPP)

Voluntary Protection Programs and on-site consultation services, when coupled with an effective enforcement program, expand employee protection to help meet the goals of the OSH Act. The VPPs motivate others to achieve excellent safety and health results in the same outstanding way as they establish a cooperative relationship between employers, employees, and OSHA.

For additional information on VPP and how to apply, contact the OSHA regional offices listed at the end of this publication.

Strategic Partnership Program

OSHA's Strategic Partnership Program, the newest member of OSHA's cooperative programs, helps encourage, assist, and recognize the efforts of partners to eliminate serious workplace hazards and achieve a high level of employee safety and health. Whereas OSHA's Consultation Program and VPP entail one-on-one relationships between OSHA and individual worksites, most strategic partnerships seek to have a broader impact by building cooperative relationships with groups of employers and employees. These partnerships are voluntary, cooperative relationships between OSHA, employers, employee representatives, and others (e.g., trade unions, trade and professional associations, universities, and other government agencies).

For more information on this and other cooperative programs, contact your nearest OSHA office, or visit OSHA's website at www.osha.gov.

Alliance Program

Through the Alliance Program, OSHA works with groups committed to safety and health, including businesses, trade or professional organizations, unions and educational institutions, to leverage resources and expertise to develop compliance assistance tools and resources and share information with employers and employees to help prevent injuries, illnesses and fatalities in the workplace.

Alliance program agreements have been established with a wide variety of industries including meat, apparel, poultry, steel, plastics, maritime, printing, chemical, construction, paper and telecommunications. These agreements are addressing many safety and health hazards and at-risk audiences, including silica, fall protection, amputations, immigrant workers, youth and small businesses. By meeting the goals of the Alliance Program agreements (training and education, outreach and communication, and promoting the national dialogue on workplace safety and health), OSHA and the Alliance Program participants are developing and disseminating compliance assistance information and resources for employers and employees such as electronic assistance tools, fact sheets, toolbox talks, and training programs.

OSHA Training and Education

OSHA area offices offer a variety of information services, such as compliance assistance, technical advice, publications, audiovisual aids, and speakers for special engagements. OSHA's Training Institute in Arlington Heights, IL, provides basic and advanced courses in safety and health for Federal and state compliance officers, state consultants, Federal agency personnel, and private sector employers, employees, and their representatives.

The OSHA Training Institute also has established OSHA Training Institute Education Centers to address the increased demand for its courses from the private sector and from other federal agencies. These centers include colleges, universities, and nonprofit training organizations that have been selected after a competition for participation in the program.

OSHA also provides funds to nonprofit organizations, through grants, to conduct workplace training and education in subjects where OSHA believes there is a lack of workplace training. Grants are awarded annually. Grant recipients are expected to contribute 20 percent of the total grant cost.

For more information on training and education, contact the OSHA Training Institute, Directorate of Training and Education, 2020 South Arlington Heights Road, Arlington Heights, IL, 60005, (847) 297-4810, or see Training on OSHA's website at www.osha.gov. For further information on any OSHA program, contact your nearest OSHA regional office listed at the end of this publication.

Information Available Electronically

OSHA has a variety of materials and tools available on its website at www.osha.gov. These include electronic compliance assistance tools, such as *Safety and Health Topics Pages, eTools, Expert Advisors;* regulations, directives, publications and videos; and other information for employers and employees. OSHA's software programs and compliance assistance tools walk you through challenging safety and health issues and common problems to find the best solutions for your workplace.

A wide variety of OSHA materials, including standards, interpretations, directives, and more can be purchased on CD-ROM from the U.S. Government Printing Office, Superintendent of Documents, toll-free phone (866) 512-1800.

OSHA Publications

OSHA has an extensive publications program. For a listing of free or sales items, visit OSHA's website at www.osha.gov or contact the OSHA Publications Office, U.S. Department of Labor, 200 Constitution Avenue, NW, N-3101, Washington, DC 20210: Telephone (202) 693-1888 or fax to (202) 693-2498.

Contacting OSHA

To report an emergency, file a complaint, or seek OSHA advice, assistance, or products, call (800) 321-OSHA or contact your nearest OSHA Regional office listed at the end of this publication. The tele-typewriter (TTY) number is (877) 889-5627.

Written correspondence can be mailed to the nearest OSHA Regional or Area Office listed at the end of this publication or to OSHA's national office at: U.S. Department of Labor, Occupational Safety and Health Administration, 200 Constitution Avenue, N.W., Washington, DC 20210.

By visiting OSHA's website at www.osha.gov, you can also:

- File a complaint online,
- Submit general inquiries about workplace safety and health electronically, and
- Find more information about OSHA and occupational safety and health.

OSHA Regional Offices

Region I
(CT,* ME, MA, NH, RI, VT*)
JFK Federal Building, Room E340
Boston, MA 02203
(617) 565-9860

Region II
(NJ,* NY,* PR,* VI*)
201 Varick Street, Room 670
New York, NY 10014
(212) 337-2378

Region III
(DE, DC, MD,* PA, VA,* WV)
The Curtis Center
170 S. Independence Mall West
Suite 740 West
Philadelphia, PA 19106-3309
(215) 861-4900

Region IV
(AL, FL, GA, KY,* MS, NC,* SC,* TN*)
61 Forsyth Street, SW, Room 6T50
Atlanta, GA 30303
(404) 562-2300

Region V
(IL, IN,* MI,* MN,* OH, WI)
230 South Dearborn Street
Room 3244
Chicago, IL 60604
(312) 353-2220

Region VI
(AR, LA, NM,* OK, TX)
525 Griffin Street, Room 602
Dallas, TX 75202
(972) 850-4145

Region VII
(IA,* KS, MO, NE)
Two Pershing Square
2300 Main Street, Suite 1010
Kansas City, MO 64108-2416
(816) 283-8745

Region VIII
(CO, MT, NO, SO, UT,* WY*)
1999 Broadway, Suite 1690
PO Box 46550
Denver, CO 80202-5716
(720) 264-6550

Region IX
(American Samoa, AZ,* CA,* HI,*
NV,* GM, Northern Mariana Islands)
90 7th Street, Suite 18-100
San Francisco, CA 94103
(415) 625-2547

Region X
(AK,* ID, OR,* WA*)
1111 Third Avenue, Suite 715
Seattle, WA 98101-3212
(206) 553-5930

* These states and territories operate their own OSHA-approved job safety and health programs and cover state and local government employees as well as private sector employees. The Connecticut, New Jersey, New York and Virgin Islands plans cover public employees only. States with approved programs must have standards that are identical to, or at least as effective as, the Federal standards.

Note: To get contact information for OSHA Area Offices, OSHA-approved State Plans and OSHA Consultation Projects, please visit us online at www.osha.gov or call us at 1-800-321-OSHA.

www.ingramcontent.com/pod-product-compliance
Lightning Source LLC
Chambersburg PA
CBHW071557170526
45166CB00004B/1708